# Eager Eaters Cookbooks

## Volume I
## Fish and Seafood

Compiled by Kelly Eager-Chism
www.EagerEatersCookbooks.com

Copyright © 2009 Eager Eaters Cookbooks

ISBN 978-0-578-00540-9

Introduction

# The History of Eager Eaters

My name is Kelly Eager-Chism, one of seven siblings and author of this, the first in a series of cookbooks entitled "Eager Eaters." Before you disappear into the delectable contents of this edition, allow me to share with you the inspiration that makes all of this possible.

I thought about all the conversations of food, recipes and restaurant offerings that always seem to be the topic of choice when our family (the clan) gets together. We all share a love affair with food. I started collecting vintage and hand-me-down recipes from family and friends and this endeavor began to take shape.

The name EAGER is not very common, and as I was thinking of a name for this cookbook series, I recalled the many nicknames and jokes that resulted from our unique last name. The one that the family laughed about the most was "Eager Eaters" and the title of the series was born. I soon realized that every family has "eager eaters" in them and what better way to celebrate this unique group than with a cookbook dedicated to the "eagerness" in all of us.

To that end, I hope you enjoy Volume I – Fish and Seafood.

# Table of Contents

**APPETIZERS** ............................................................... 7

Clam Dip .................................................................. 8

Crab Rangoon Pizza Bites ................................................. 9

Crab Stuffing ............................................................ 10

Crabmeat Cheese Puffs ................................................... 11

Lafayette Shrimp or Crab Claws ........................................... 12

Shrimp Mousse ............................................................ 13

Shrimp Spread ............................................................ 14

Tuna Tar Tar ............................................................. 15

**CASSEROLES** ............................................................. 17

Chinese Buffet Crab Casserole ............................................ 18

Crab Casserole ........................................................... 19

Halibut Fillets Au Gratin ................................................ 20

Oyster Stuffing .......................................................... 21

Seafood Quiche ........................................................... 22

Shrimp Enchiladas ........................................................ 23

| | |
|---|---|
| ENTREES | 25 |
| Bubba Gump's Shrimpin' Dippin' Broth | 26 |
| Crab Cakes | 27 |
| Dirty Shrimp | 28 |
| Fabulous Flounder Florentine | 29 |
| Fiery Shrimp | 30 |
| Grits A Ya-Ya | 32 |
| McGuire's Crab Cakes | 34 |
| Oyster Stew | 36 |
| Pan Fried Rainbow Trout | 37 |
| Peel and Eat Shrimp | 38 |
| Pepper Shrimp | 39 |
| Polly's Perfect Salmon | 40 |
| Salmon with Tomato and Herb Topping | 41 |
| Seared Scallops with Wilted Spinach | 42 |
| Shrimp Creole | 43 |
| Southern Fried Shrimp or Oysters | 44 |
| Tangy Lemon Broiled Fish | 45 |
| Trout Amandine | 46 |
| Tuna Cakes | 47 |

# APPETIZERS

# Clam Dip

*Got a party coming up? Here's a quick and easy dip to prepare for your guests. Make it ahead of time and refrigerate it overnight to give the seasonings time to marry.*

1 can (8 ounces) minced clams, drained, reserving juice

1 pkg (8 ounces) cream cheese, softened

2 teaspoons lemon juice

2 teaspoons chili sauce

2 teaspoons Worcestershire sauce

1/2 teaspoon salt

1/8 teaspoon ground black pepper

Dash of hot sauce

Paprika

In a small mixing bowl, combine everything except the clam juice and the paprika. Using an electric beater or wire whisk, blend till smooth. If too thick for dipping, add clam juice one tablespoon at a time till you reach the desired consistency. Fold in the minced clams. Pour into serving bowl, and sprinkle with paprika. Serve with salted bagel chips or crackers of choice.

Serves 6-8.

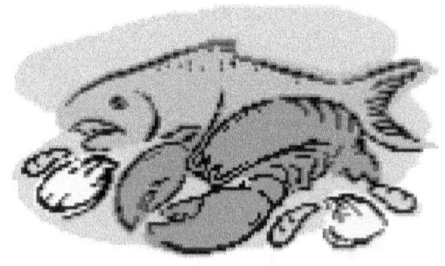

# Crab Rangoon Pizza Bites

*Here's a variation of the popular Chinese buffet side dish. Instead of being wrapped in a won ton wrapper or phyllo dough, the filling is spread on English muffins.*

6 English muffins, split to yield 12 halves

1 pkg (8 ounces) low fat cream cheese, softened

1/4 cup mayonnaise

1/4 teaspoon garlic salt

2 teaspoons sugar

1 can (8 ounces) sliced water chestnuts, drained & coarsely chopped

1 can (6 ounces) lump crabmeat, drained & shell fragments removed

1/4 cup crushed pineapple, drained well

2 cups (8 ounces) shredded Monterey Jack cheese

2 chopped green onions, green part only (about 3 Tablespoons)

Place muffin halves on ungreased cookie sheet, cut side up. In a medium bowl, beat cream cheese, mayonnaise, garlic salt and sugar with electric mixer until smooth. Fold in water chestnuts, crabmeat and pineapple. Spread mixture over muffin halves. Sprinkle with cheese and green onions. With a sharp knife, cut muffins into fourths. Leave on cookie sheet and freeze. When frozen, place cut pieces in freezer bag for later use. **(Note: these are best when baked from this frozen state.)**

To cook, preheat oven to 350 degrees. Place desired number of frozen pieces on foil lined cookie sheet and bake for approximately 10-15 minutes or until slightly browned. Serve warm.

Yields 48 pieces.

# Crab Stuffing

*There is a vast difference in the taste and texture of fresh (or canned) crabmeat versus the artificial crab. Crab meat is plentiful on the Gulf Coast so why default to something artificial?*

1 pound crabmeat, shell fragments removed

1/2 cup mayonnaise

3 Tablespoons lemon juice

3 Tablespoons Worcestershire sauce

2 Tablespoons Dijon-style mustard

1 teaspoon ground black pepper

Salt to taste

In a small bowl, combine all ingredients. Use to stuff baked fish, baked or fried butterflied shrimp or top your favorite cracker as an appetizer.

Yields about 2 1/2 cups.

# Crabmeat Cheese Puffs *submitted by Kelly Chism*

*This is really easy and it will be a hit with your guests! Make ahead for large dinner parties or keep on hand in the freezer as a quick appetizer or luncheon entrée for unexpected company. Just heat and serve.*

1 pkg English muffins, split to yield 12 halves

1 can (6 ounces) crabmeat, drained, shell fragments removed

1 pkg (8 ounces) cream cheese, softened

1 jar (5 ounces) Kraft Old English cheese, room temperature

4 Tablespoons (1/2 stick) margarine or butter, softened

2 1/2 Tablespoons mayonnaise

1/4 teaspoon garlic salt

1/4 teaspoon garlic powder

Dash of ground red pepper or hot sauce (optional)

Old Bay Seasoning or paprika for color or more taste

Place muffin halves on ungreased cookie sheet. In a medium mixing bowl, combine next 7 (or 8) ingredients and cream together. Spread onto English muffins. Sprinkle lightly with paprika or Old Bay seafood seasoning. With a sharp knife, cut muffins into fourths. Leave on cookie sheet and freeze. When frozen, place cut pieces in freezer bag for later use. **(Note: these are best when baked from this frozen state.)**

To cook, preheat oven to 350 degrees. Place desired number of frozen pieces on foil lined cookie sheet and bake for approximately 10-15 minutes or until slightly browned. Serve warm.

Yields 48 pieces.

# Lafayette Shrimp or Crab Claws

*My hubby, Bob, and I discovered this crab dish at a local restaurant. The sherry and heavy cream are the secrets to this wonderful dipping dish. This is delicious with crispy baked French bread for dipping – you'll want to sop up every drop.*

4 Tablespoons olive oil
12 shrimp (heads & shells removed, tails intact)
    or 32 blue crab claws (loose fragments removed)
2 Tablespoons blackened fish seasoning
1 1/2 teaspoons minced, minced
1 1/2 teaspoons diced shallots
1/4 cup white wine
1/2 cup dry sherry
1/4 cup hot sauce
2 teaspoons Worcestershire sauce
1 1/2 teaspoons Creole mustard
3/4 cup heavy whipping cream
1 Tablespoon butter

Heat olive oil in a medium skillet over medium-high heat. Add shrimp or crab claws. Sprinkle with blackened fish seasoning, garlic and shallots. Sauté for approximately 30 seconds. Deglaze pan with white wine and sherry. Remove seafood and set aside. To the skillet, add hot sauce, Worcestershire sauce and mustard. Reduce to a paste-like consistency, stirring frequently. Add heavy cream and reduce to sauce consistency, stirring frequently. Return seafood to the sauce. Turn off the heat and add butter. Stir until incorporated.

Serves 2.

# Shrimp Mousse *submitted by Jean Eager*

*This spread is prepared in a fish shaped salad mold. Part of the fun of this party food is decorating the fish! Use a stuffed olive slice for the eye and maybe thin lemon peel or green pepper strips to simulate scales.*

1 envelope (1/4 ounce) unflavored gelatin

1 can (10.5 ounces) condensed tomato soup

1 pkg (8 ounces) cream cheese, softened

1/4 cup minced sweet onion

1 cup mayonnaise

1/2 cup minced celery

1 pound shrimp, cooked and minced

Dissolve gelatin in 1/3 cup water. In a saucepan, over low heat, bring condensed tomato soup **(do not dilute with water)** to a boil. Add gelatin and stir. In a blender, combine cream cheese, soup/gelatin mixture and minced onion. Pour mixture into a bowl and allow to cool. Whisk in mayonnaise and celery. Fold in shrimp. "Mush" together. *(Mom says, "Mush rhymes with push.")* Prepare a fish shaped mold by wiping the inside with mayonnaise. Pour in mixture, cover with plastic wrap and chill overnight. When ready to serve, invert onto a lettuce-lined platter. (If mousse does not easily release, sink the mold in hot water for just a few seconds, as deep as possible without getting water on the food. Invert onto platter.) Decorate and serve with crackers of your choice.

Serves 16.

# Shrimp Spread

*This recipe came from my Aunt Lynn (Jean Eager's sister) in 1983. It's very similar to the Clam Dip earlier in this book with some variations. If it was easy, Aunt Lynn knew how to do it.*

1 pkg (8 ounces) Neufchatel cheese (or cream cheese), softened

1/4 cup mayonnaise

2 Tablespoons chopped sweet onion

1 teaspoon Worcestershire sauce

2 Tablespoons chili sauce

1/4 teaspoon hot sauce

1/2 teaspoons lemon juice

1 can (4 ounces) baby shrimp, drained
      or 1/4 pound fresh shrimp, cooked, shelled and deveined

Put all ingredients into a food processor and blend till smooth. Pour into a serving dish. Cover with plastic wrap and chill at least two hours. When ready to serve, garnish with fresh parsley and serve with crackers.

Serves 6-8.

# Tuna Tar Tar

*If you like sushi, you're going to love this. It takes just minutes to prepare and your friends will think you got it from a five star restaurant. It's amazingly simple with an outstanding flavor!*

1 pound sushi grade tuna, finely diced

3 Tablespoons olive oil

1/4 teaspoon wasabi powder

1 Tablespoon sesame seeds

1/8 teaspoon coarsely ground black pepper

French baguette, sliced thin

In a bowl, stir together olive oil, wasabi powder, sesame seeds and black pepper. Toss raw tuna in the mixture until evenly coated. Adjust seasoning as desired. Place bread slices on a cookie sheet. Lightly spread each with butter. Broil till golden brown. Serve with tar tar as a great little appetizer.

Serves 12.

# CASSEROLES

# Chinese Buffet Crab Casserole

*This is a low-fat version of a similar casserole found on many Chinese restaurant buffets. I always head for it first when I'm hungry for seafood! I can't decide if this is more of a soufflé or a deep dish crustless quiche. Either way, it's a great dish for brunch!*

16 ounces imitation crabmeat, coarsely shredded

2 eggs, whites and yolks separated

1 1/2 cups white sauce, made with non-fat milk*

2 Tablespoons finely chopped green pepper

1/2 teaspoon hot sauce

1/2 cup shredded reduced-fat cheddar cheese

Salt and pepper to taste

1/2 cup shredded reduced-fat cheddar cheese for topping

Preheat oven to 325 degrees. Prepare a small oven proof baking dish with non-stick cooking spray.

Separate eggs into two different bowls. Beat yolks till buttery color. Prepare white sauce and slowly pour in beaten egg yolks stirring constantly. With clean beaters, whip egg whites till foamy. Fold beaten egg whites, green pepper, hot sauce and 1/2 cup of cheese into the white sauce/egg yolk mixture. Pour into prepared baking dish. Sprinkle remaining 1/2 cup cheese on top. Bake uncovered for 30 minutes.

Serves 4.

*\*To make 1 ½ cups of white sauce, melt 1 ½ tablespoons of margarine or butter in a saucepan over medium heat. Add 1 ½ tablespoons of flour and stir to make a paste. Add 1 ½ cups of non-fat milk and whisk constantly until hot and creamy. Remove from heat.*

# Crab Casserole

*Sinfully rich and delicious, this can be served as a casserole or as a dip/spread.*

1 Tablespoon butter
1/2 cup chopped sweet onion
1/2 cup chopped, red or green bell pepper
1/2 cup crushed crackers (your choice)
1 pkg (8 ounces) cream cheese, softened
1 cup (8 ounces) sour cream
1/4 cup mayonnaise
1 Tablespoon Worcestershire sauce
1/2 teaspoon hot sauce
1 teaspoon Old Bay Seasoning
1/2 teaspoon paprika
1/4 teaspoon garlic powder
1/4 teaspoon ground black pepper
Salt to taste
1 pound lump crabmeat, shell fragments removed
1 cup grated cheddar or Gouda cheese (brown rind removed)

Preheat oven to 350 degrees. Prepare a 2 ½ - 3 quart oven proof baking dish with non-stick cooking spray.

In a skillet or saucepan, melt butter. Sauté onions and peppers over medium heat until tender; stir in the crushed crackers; remove from heat. In a mixing bowl, beat together cream cheese, sour cream, Worcestershire, hot sauce, and dry seasonings. Stir in the sautéed onion/pepper/cracker mixture. Gently fold in the crabmeat, being careful not to break up the lumps too much. Pour into prepared baking dish. Bake uncovered for 20 minutes. Remove from oven and stir gently. Sprinkle cheese on top and return to oven for another 10 minutes.

Serves 6.

## Halibut Fillets Au Gratin, *submitted by Jen Chism*

*This recipe was presented to Jennifer Chism during her wedding shower. It was a gift from Pat Morris, long time friend of the family.*

1 pound halibut fillets

1 Tablespoon fine cracker crumbs

1 can (14.5 ounces) diced tomatoes with liquid

1 Tablespoon chopped onion

1/4 teaspoon salt

Black pepper to taste

1 Tablespoon butter

4 ounces cheddar cheese, shredded

Preheat oven to 375 degrees. Prepare a baking dish with non-stick cooking spray.

Sprinkle prepared baking dish with crumbs. Arrange halibut on top of crumbs. In a small bowl, combine tomatoes, onions, salt and pepper. Pour over fillets. Dot with butter. Bake uncovered for 20 minutes. Sprinkle with cheese and return to oven until cheese melts.

Serves 4.

# Oyster Stuffing

*Here's a great alternative stuffing for your holiday bird or it's just as good baked in a casserole dish.*

1 pound bread, slightly dried and cubed (10 cups packed)
1 pint raw oysters (drain and reserve the liquor)
6 Tablespoons butter
1 cup finely chopped celery
2 cups chopped onions
1/4 cup parsley flakes
1 Tablespoon sage
1 Tablespoon thyme
3/4 teaspoon salt
1/2 teaspoon ground black pepper
1/4 teaspoon ground nutmeg
1/8 teaspoon ground clove
1 cup oyster liquor or chicken stock
2 eggs, beaten

Preheat oven to 350 degrees. Prepare an oven proof baking dish with non-stick cooking spray.

On an ungreased baking sheet, spread out the bread cubes. Toast until golden brown, tossing as necessary. Pour into a large bowl. In a large skillet, heat butter until melted and foam subsides. Add celery and onions and cook about 5 minutes or until tender. Remove from heat and stir in the spices. Slowly pour over the bread cubes and toss. Add oysters, stock and eggs. Gently mix until the stuffing is moist, but not packed together. Stuff cavity of bird 3/4 full. Pour remaining dressing into the prepared baking dish. Bake uncovered 25-30 minutes until heated through and a crust begins to form on the outside. (If baked as a casserole only, you may have to bake an additional 15 minutes.) Serves 8.

## Seafood Quiche *submitted by family friend, Eileen Brotherton*

*My hubby Bob, and I have shared many a meal with the Brothertons. This was served for a brunch at one of our celebrations.*

4 Tablespoons unsalted butter
1 bunch chopped green onions, green only
2 cans (6 ounces each) lump crabmeat, drained and shell fragments removed
1 pkg (12 ounces) pre-cooked frozen shrimp
1 pound scallops, lightly poached
2 Tablespoons dry sherry
1 11-inch pie shell, partially baked
1/2 cup Swiss cheese, grated
3 large eggs
1 cup heavy cream
1/4 teaspoon salt
Pinch of white pepper

Thaw shrimp according to package directions. Thaw scallops according to directions and poach in lightly salted water. In a large skillet, melt butter and sauté green onions until soft. Add crabmeat, shrimp, scallops and sherry. Bring to a boil, remove from heat and allow to cool.

Preheat oven to 375 degrees.

Pour cooled seafood into pie shell and top with grated cheese. In a large bowl, combine eggs, cream, salt and pepper. Beat well and pour over cheese layer. Bake for approximately 30 minutes or until set. Knife blade inserted in the middle will come out clean when done.

Serves 4-6.

# Shrimp Enchiladas

*My family loves Mexican food and fresh seafood. What could be better than combining the two in this great seafood enchilada dish? By combining a rich white sauce and a mild enchilada sauce, the taste of the shrimp is still evident and not overpowered by the sauce. Serve with a side of shredded lettuce, sour cream and/or guacamole.*

3 Tablespoons unsalted butter, divided
1/2 cup chopped onion
1 green bell pepper, cored, seeded and sliced into thin strips
2 cloves minced garlic
1 pound fully cooked shrimp, shelled, deveined and coarsely chopped
2 Tablespoons flour
1 cup half and half
1 can (10 ounces) mild enchilada sauce
1 cup (4 ounces) shredded mild cheddar cheese, divided
8 small flour tortillas

Preheat oven at 375 degrees. Prepare a 9x13 baking dish with nonstick cooking spray.

In a large skillet over medium high heat, melt 1 tablespoon butter. Add onion, peppers and garlic and cook 7 minutes, until softened. Stir in the shrimp. Remove from heat and let cool slightly. In a small saucepan over medium heat, melt the remaining 2 tablespoons butter. Sprinkle with flour and whisk until smooth. Whisk in half and half and continue to cook over medium-high heat until thickened, about 5 minutes. Stir in enchilada sauce, whisking continuously until blended. Remove sauce from heat and stir ¾ cup of the sauce and ¼ cup of the shredded cheese into the shrimp mixture.

(continued)

Spoon about 1/3 cup shrimp mixture down center of one tortilla. Roll tightly to enclose filling, then transfer to prepared dish, seam side down. Repeat with remaining tortillas and filling. Pour remaining sauce over enchiladas, spreading to the edges. Top with remaining shredded cheese. Bake uncovered for 20 minutes, until cheese is melted and sauce is bubbly. Cool slightly before serving.

Serves 4.

*You could substitute artificial crab and Monterey Jack cheese and have a different but equally good taste. Just keep the sauce on the mild side.*

# ENTREES

# Bubba Gump's Shrimpin' Dippin' Broth

a Copycat recipe

*My hubby, Bob, and I enjoyed this menu treat while at Navy Pier in Chicago. Find a Bubba Gump's near you!!! It's got a casual, fun atmosphere you'll love! Oh, the food is great too! This broth goes together **very quickly**. To avoid rubbery overcooked shrimp, start rice first and slide French bread into preheated oven before starting the dippin' broth.*

1 stick (1/4 pound) real butter (unsalted if possible)

1/8 teaspoon hot sauce

1 Tablespoon Worcestershire sauce

1 Tablespoon ground black pepper

1 teaspoon garlic powder

1 teaspoon Old Bay Seasoning

32 ounces clam juice

2 pounds shrimp, shelled, deveined and rinsed

Melt butter in bottom of a large pot. (Don't skimp on the butter. One stick is minimum.) Add sauces and seasonings. Stir well. Add shrimp and cook for *only 1 minute* over medium heat (shrimp will begin to curl and look pink on the edges). Add clam juice and bring to a boil. *Simmer one minute and remove from heat.*

Serve in a bowl over a scoop of fluffy white rice and slices of crunchy, warm French bread on the side for dipping.

Serves 4.

*Personally I find the salt in the Worcestershire, seasoning and the clam juice to be enough, but add salt if you desire.*

# Crab Cakes

*Living on the Gulf Coast, fresh seafood is readily available. These mouth-watering cakes contain crabmeat, onion, pepper and spices. It's a very satisfying cake and would be a perfect compliment to a crisp green salad.*

1 pound fresh lump crabmeat, shell fragments removed
    (or canned crabmeat, drained and shell fragments removed)

1/3 cup seasoned breadcrumbs

3 finely chopped green onions, green and white parts

1/2 cup finely chopped red bell pepper

1/4 cup mayonnaise

1 egg, beaten

1 teaspoon Worcestershire sauce

1 teaspoon dry mustard

1 Tablespoon lemon juice

Dash of ground red pepper

Flour for dusting

1/2 cup olive oil

In a large bowl, mix all ingredients, except flour & oil. Shape into patties and dust with flour. Make 4 large patties for entrée portions, or smaller for appetizers. *NOTE: Can be frozen at this point.*

Heat oil in a large skillet over medium heat. (If it starts to smoke, it's too hot.) Carefully slide in the crab cakes so they are not touching each other and fry until browned, about 4-5 minutes on each side. Drain on paper towel. Serve hot with your favorite remoulade or tartar sauce.

Serves 4.

# Dirty Shrimp

*You've heard of dirty rice, but have you heard of dirty shrimp before? Pop two cans of your favorite brewsky for this one - one for the recipe and one for you.*

2 pounds large shrimp, shelled and deveined

4 Tablespoons butter

2 teaspoons minced garlic

1 teaspoon dried oregano

1 teaspoon dried basil

1 teaspoon dried thyme

1 teaspoon ground red pepper

1/2 teaspoon crushed red pepper flakes

1/4 teaspoon salt

1/4 teaspoon ground black pepper

1/2 cup beer

In a large skillet, melt butter and sauté garlic and next seven herbs until garlic is slightly golden but not browned. Add shrimp, stirring constantly, until shrimp are pink and cooked through. Pour in beer, simmer 1 minute more, and serve!

Serves 5-6.

# Fabulous Flounder Florentine

*Have you had your daily serving of a green leafy vegetable today? This is just too easy.*

2 pkgs (10 ounces each) frozen chopped spinach
1/4 cup minced onion
4 Tablespoons butter or margarine, melted, divided
2 pounds flounder fillets*
2 teaspoons lemon juice
1/2 cup milk
2 cups grated processed American cheese

Preheat broiler. Prepare a 9x13 oven proof baking dish with non-stick cooking spray.

Cook spinach as directed on package, drain**. In a small skillet, melt 2 tablespoons butter. Add minced onion and sauté until translucent, not brown. Add drained spinach and toss. Place fish fillets in the prepared baking dish. Dot with remaining butter. Sprinkle with lemon juice. Broil, 2 inches from heat for 8-10 minutes or until easily flaked with a fork and still moist. Spoon spinach mixture in between and around fish fillets. In a saucepan over medium heat, heat milk. Add cheese and stir until smooth. Pour cheese sauce over all. Broil 4 inches from heat until golden.

Serves 6.

*\* Other mild flavored, delicate to medium textured fish fillets like haddock, cod, tilapia and grouper may be substituted for the flounder.*

*\*\* TIP from AJ. When she drains spinach, instead of squeezing by hand, she puts it on a clean dry kitchen towel (with a layer of paper towel) and wrings out the water! Cool!*

# Fiery Shrimp *submitted by Kelly Chism*

*I saw this recipe in a very old USA Weekend in which the featured celebrity cook was Jill St. John. It has become my signature dish for company. Guests can't get enough of it! Although the shrimp is heavenly, the dipping sauce is peppery hot and divine. Serve with hot crunchy French baguettes. If you are really hungry, add a spinach salad. Yum!*

2 sticks butter

2 sticks margarine

1/2 cup Worcestershire sauce

4 Tablespoons finely ground black pepper

    (That's right! 4 Tablespoons. **Avoid coarse ground pepper.**)

1 teaspoon rosemary

2 teaspoons hot sauce

2 teaspoons salt

3 cloves minced garlic

Juice of 2 lemons (5 Tablespoons)

5 pounds headless shrimp, rinsed and drained

2 lemons, thinly sliced

Preheat oven to 400 degrees.

In a saucepan, melt butter and margarine. Stir in remaining ingredients except for the shrimp and sliced lemons and set aside. In a large baking/serving dish, arrange shrimp, overlapping as you go, to make an attractive arrangement.* Randomly insert lemon slices between the shrimps. Pour melted butter mixture evenly over the shrimp and lemons. Bake uncovered 15-20 minutes (depending on size of shrimp).

(continued)

Place the baking dish in middle of your table. The broth is rich with butter and garlic and spicy with lots of black pepper taste. Encourage guests to dip crusty French bread till the "soppy" is gone. (It gets even better toward the bottom of the dish!)

Serves about 8.

*I make this in a large round cooking pan. I line up the shrimp just inside the perimeter of the pan, all facing the same way, tails to the center. Then I make another concentric circle of shrimp inside and overlapping the first, then another and another until all the tails reach the center of the dish. It's very artsy looking. The tucked in lemon slices add color and flavor. It's a great presentation!*

# Grits A Ya-Ya

*This is the signature dish from The Fish House, a local restaurant in Pensacola. Chef Jim Shirley is the creator of this awesome dish. Serve up healthy portions of the Smoked Gouda Grits and top with a small ladle of the shrimp/spinach sauce. The grits are the star in this recipe.*

8 strips bacon, diced

1 Tablespoon minced garlic

1 Tablespoon minced shallots

3 Tablespoons butter

Splash of white wine

1 pound jumbo shrimp, peeled and deveined

1 large Portobello mushroom cap, sliced

1/4 cup diced green onion, green only

2 cups chopped fresh spinach

2 cups heavy cream

3 cups Smoked Gouda Cheese Grits (recipe follows)

Salt, pepper and hot sauce to taste

Heat a large saucepan over medium heat. Add bacon and stir-fry for 3 minutes to render bacon grease and bacon is at least translucent. Add garlic and shallots and sauté until soft but not browned. Add butter and a splash of white wine. When the butter is half melted, add the shrimp. When the undersides of the shrimp become white, flip them and add mushrooms, green onions and spinach. Sauté for 2 minutes. Remove the shrimp. Pour in the heavy cream and let simmer, occasionally stirring. When reduced by one third, add salt, pepper and hot sauce to taste. Return shrimp to the sauce and stir. Spoon the sauce onto heaping mounds of Gouda Grits.

Serves 4.

## Smoked Gouda Cheese Grits

*The original recipe from the Fish House was enough to feed a small army. I have quartered the recipe to serve 4 people, and lowering sodium and fat.*

1 can (10.5 ounces) low sodium chicken broth

3/4 cup water

2 cups fat-free half and half

3/4 cup quick grits (not instant)

1 Tablespoon butter

4 ounces shredded smoked Gouda cheese (remove brown rind)

In a large saucepan, combine chicken stock, water and half and half. Bring to a boil. Add grits and cook on medium-high for 5 minutes, stirring frequently. Add butter and cook on low heat for 10 minutes. Add smoked Gouda cheese and stir till smooth.

# McGuire's Crab Cakes

*McGuire's is a five star Irish pub and brewery in Pensacola. They submitted this recipe on the occasion of the 2005 Fiesta Seafood Grille. In this recipe, the ingredients are kept to a minimum. It's full of lump crabmeat and makes a very attractive presentation.*

1 pound jumbo lump crabmeat, shell fragments removed

3/4 cup bread crumbs

1 egg, beaten

Pinch of salt and pepper

1/2 cup flour

1 Tablespoon olive oil

2 Tablespoons lemon juice

2 cups spring mix

1/2 lemon, thinly sliced and twisted

8 sliced piquante peppers (optional)

1 cup Remoulade sauce (recipe follows)

In a medium bowl, gently combine crabmeat, bread crumbs, egg, salt and pepper. Form into four patties. Dredge each patty on both sides with flour. Preheat a non-stick skillet with 1 tablespoon olive oil. Brown the cakes on both sides and drain on paper towel. (Drizzle pan with more oil if necessary.) Place spring mix in the middle of a salad plate. Place crab cakes on side of spring mix and top with Remoulade sauce. (Recipe follows.) Garnish with lemon twists and sliced piquante peppers.

Serves 4.

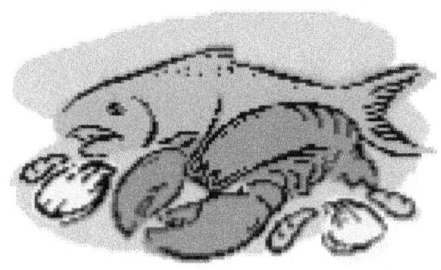

## Southern Living's Remoulade Sauce

3 Tablespoons prepared horseradish*

1/2 cup tarragon vinegar

2 Tablespoons ketchup

1 Tablespoons paprika

1 teaspoon salt

1 clove garlic

1 cup vegetable oil

1/2 cup chopped green onions (green only)

1/2 cup chopped celery

1/2 teaspoon ground red pepper

Place all ingredients in blender and blend thoroughly.

*There IS a difference in the quality of horseradish. For texture and heat, I recommend Zatarin's if you can find it. It's usually in the refrigerated section near the cheese case. If 3 Tablespoons isn't hot enough for you, add more to desired taste.

# Oyster Stew

*Oysters can be readily found along the Gulf Coast (except after a hurricane). They are best harvested in months that have an "r" in them. Raw oysters or baked oysters are great too, but here's a hearty stew sure to please. Many families enjoy this stew as part of their Christmas Eve tradition.*

1/4 cup butter
1 cup minced celery
3 Tablespoons minced shallots
1 pint freshly shucked oysters with strained "liquor" *
1 quart whole milk
1 quart fat-free half and half
Salt and ground black pepper to taste
Pinch of ground red pepper
1/4 cup sherry (optional)

In a small saucepan, melt butter. Cook celery and shallots until tender. Add oysters with liquor. Cook and stir over low heat just until edges of oysters curl. Remove from heat. **In another saucepan** heat milk and half and half. To avoid curdling, do **not** bring to a boil. Stir in salt and peppers. Add oysters. Stir in sherry **a little at a time** to be sure you like the flavor. Ladle into shallow bowls. Serve with crusty bread or oyster crackers.

Serves 4.

* Oyster liquor, also called oyster liquid, is the salty juice from the oyster that runs off during the shucking process. It is used when packing fresh oysters into pint or quart containers. Chicken or seafood stock, or canned clam juice, are all great substitutes.

*Like many soups and stews, this is better if prepared the day before. When reheating, be sure to use LOW heat.*

# Pan Fried Rainbow Trout

*I have fond memories of the smell of the fish that my grandfather cooked. We vacationed at a family cottage in Star Lake, New York. The kitchen was galley-style and very small. My grandfather built an outdoor grill, specifically for cooking fish. When he cooked fresh fish, there was a "mess" of it!*

4 whole trout with heads, gutted
1/3 cup flour
1/3 cup cornmeal
1 teaspoon salt
1 teaspoon ground red pepper
1/4 teaspoon garlic powder (optional)
4 Tablespoons butter or vegetable oil
Lemon juice, optional

Rinse the fish, inside and out, under cold running water but do not scrub. The natural film helps the flour adhere to the fish. In a shallow bowl, combine flour, cornmeal and spices. Melt the butter in a large heavy skillet over medium-high heat. Dredge the trout in the flour mixture and shake off the excess. When the butter is melted, place the trout in the skillet. Cook 4-5 minutes on each side or until the coating is golden brown and the skin is crispy. Drizzle with lemon juice if desired. Serve hot.

Serves 4.

*Never eaten whole trout? If you're squeamish about the fish eyes "looking at you", remove heads before cooking. When cooked, the skin is edible and the crispy tails are very tasty. The skeletal structure of trout makes it a very easy fish to eat. Pull off any fins. Make a horizontal incision right along the length of the fish, from the gills to the tail, equidistant between the back and the belly. The flesh will pull away easily with a fork. When you've eaten the first side, insert a knife under the spade-shaped bone near the tail. Wiggle the knife until the bone comes away from the flesh. Grab the tail between your fingers and pull it gently away. It should come away intact, with the head. Who knew?*

# Peel and Eat Shrimp

*You can't live on the Gulf Coast and not enjoy the fresh bounty of the sea. A trip to the local seafood market where the fish is unloaded directly from the boats, dressed and thrown on ice is an experience. A visit to Patti's Seafood is on everybody's list of things to see while in Pensacola. Believe it or not, Patti's Seafood is one of our city's tourist attractions! Be sure to try the Royal Reds when they are available. Royal Red Shrimp are a deep water bright red shrimp caught mostly off of Florida's Coast and a few places in the Gulf of Mexico. They are the sweetest shrimp. The highly prized flavor is unique and highly sought after.*

1 can (12 ounces) beer
2 1/2 pounds medium shrimp, heads and shells
1/4 cup Old Bay seasoning
Lemon wedges

Into a large pot, pour 2" of water and contents of one can of beer. Bring to a boil. Add shrimp and sprinkle on Old Bay seasoning. Do not stir. Instead, shuffle shrimp gently to disperse seasoning. Cover and steam for 5 minutes, until shrimp is firm and cooked through. Serve shrimp in their shells with lemon wedges, and melted butter with Old Bay seasoning for dipping.

Serves 5.

*Be sure to put a "bone bowl" on the table for the heads and shells.*

# Pepper Shrimp

*Often found on a Chinese buffet, this is about as easy as it gets. Traditionally though, this spicy shrimp is served on newspaper, like English fish and chips.*

2 pounds jumbo headless shrimp

2 cups cold water

2 1/2 Tablespoons lemon juice

1 1/2 Tablespoons ground black pepper

1 Tablespoons paprika

1 Tablespoon butter

In a large saucepan, place shrimp, water and lemon juice. Sprinkle with pepper and paprika. Dot with butter. Bring to boil. Remove saucepan from heat and turn over shrimp. Let stand in hot liquid 3-4 minutes. Drain shrimp and transfer to serving dish. Sprinkle with remaining 1 1/2 teaspoons of black pepper and 1 Tablespoon of paprika. Toss well and serve.

Serves 4.

## **Polly's Perfect Salmon**, *submitted by Polly Burge, friend of the family*

*This interesting process of cooking salmon involves mayonnaise and it's the oil in the mayonnaise that makes this recipe work. Do not substitute low fat or non fat mayonnaise. It's just not the same.*

1 pound of salmon

1/4 cup mayonnaise

Salt and pepper

1 teaspoon dried parsley

2 1/2 Tablespoons lemon juice

Dash of paprika

Preheat oven to 425 degrees. Prepare an oven proof baking dish by lining it with aluminum foil.

Rinse the salmon and dry it off with a paper towel. Place it skin side down on the aluminum foil. Spread mayonnaise to all exposed salmon. Sprinkle with salt and pepper, parsley, lemon juice, and a dash of paprika. Bake uncovered for 20-22 minutes. With a pancake turner, lift salmon from the foil and remove to a serving platter. You'll find that the skin is left behind on the foil. Roll up the foil and discard. Magic!

Serves 2-3.

*A firm white fish may be substituted for the salmon. If using something like grouper or snapper or mahi mahi, spray the aluminum foil with non-stick cooking spray.*

# Salmon with Tomato and Herb Topping

*A picture is worth a 1000 words. You've got to see this elegant dish to believe it!*

1/3 cup seeded and chopped vine-ripened tomatoes

1/3 cup julienne-sliced sun-dried tomatoes, packed in oil

2 Tablespoons olive oil

2 teaspoons dried oregano

2 Tablespoons chopped green onion (green only)

1 teaspoon minced garlic

Freshly ground black pepper, to taste

1 pound salmon fillet, approximately 1 inch thick

Prepare a shallow baking dish with nonstick spray.

In a mixing bowl, combine all ingredients except salmon. Mix well. Place salmon, skin side down, in prepared dish. Spoon tomato mixture evenly over salmon. *Cover and refrigerate at least 4 hours until ready to cook.*

Preheat oven to 375 degrees. Bake uncovered, 30 minutes or until fish flakes easily. (Cooking time varies depending on thickness of fillet.)

Serves 2-3.

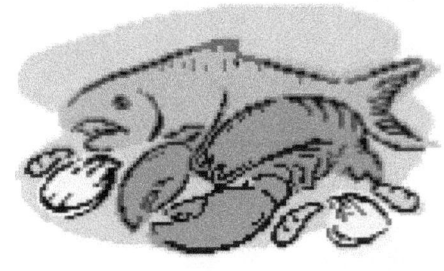

# Seared Scallops with Wilted Spinach

*Scallops, spinach and balsamic vinegar? Don't knock it till you've tried it!*

1 pound fresh sea scallops, sliced in half horizontally

2 Tablespoons flour

2 teaspoons blackened fish seasoning

2 Tablespoons vegetable or olive oil

1 pkg (10 ounces) prewashed baby spinach leaves

1/2 cup julienned carrots

2 1/2 Tablespoons balsamic vinegar

1 Tablespoon water

Rinse scallops and pat dry. In a zippered plastic bag, combine flour and seasoning. Add dry scallops and toss to coat. Heat oil in a large skillet over medium heat. Sauté scallops for 3-5 minutes or until browned and opaque, turning once. Remove scallops and keep warm. Add spinach and carrots to skillet. Sprinkle with water to create steam. Cover and cook over medium-high heat about 2 minutes or until spinach starts to wilt. Add vinegar. Toss to coat evenly. Spoon spinach onto plates. Top with scallops.

Serves 4.

# Shrimp Creole

*Pensacola is only a few hours from New Orleans. Mardi Gras has found its way here as an annual celebration with parties and parades. But more importantly, it has made Creole and Cajun cooking common in our area.*

1 pound shrimp, cooked and peeled
1/4 cup butter or margarine
1/2 cup chopped onion
1/2 cup chopped celery
1/3 cup chopped green bell pepper
3 Tablespoons flour
2 1/2 cups tomatoes, sieved
1 bay leaf
1 Tablespoon dried parsley
1 1/2 teaspoons salt
1 teaspoon sugar
3/4 teaspoon Worcestershire sauce
1/2 teaspoon ground black pepper
2-3 drops hot sauce
2 cups cooked, fluffy white rice

In a large skillet over medium-high heat, melt butter or margarine. Add onion, celery and green pepper. Sauté until onion is transparent and other vegetables are tender. Add flour and stir until bubbly. While stirring, gradually add tomatoes and all seasonings. Cover and simmer 30 minutes. **Remove bay leaf.** Add shrimp and stir. Cover, reduce het to low and cook until heated through. To serve, ladle into shallow bowls. Put a scoop of rice in the center. Garnish with parsley. Serve with warm crunchy French bread.

Serves 4-6.

# Southern Fried Shrimp or Oysters

*Golden and seasoned just right! Try these with fries and slaw. Oh, y'all!*

12 shrimp, butterflied or 12 oysters, shucked and drained

3 eggs

4 Tablespoons hot sauce

1 cup flour

1 teaspoon salt

1/2 teaspoon ground black pepper

1/2 teaspoon garlic powder

Vegetable oil for frying

In a deep bowl, whip eggs with hot sauce. In another bowl, combine flour, salt, pepper, and garlic powder. Mix well. Dip each shrimp or oyster in egg mixture then toss in the seasoned flour till completely coated (press with fingers to make flour hold). Place on plate till ready to fry. (Refrigerate if you have prepared these ahead of time.)

In a deep fryer or deep saucepan pour about 2" oil. Preheat oil to 375 degrees. Maintain temperature of oil throughout. Drop one at a time into hot oil. Do not crowd the surface of the oil. Fry till golden brown, turning once. Remove with slotted spoon and drain on paper towel.

*To use the shrimp or oysters in Po-Boys, slice a quality French roll in half lengthwise. Butter the bread and broil till golden brown. Layer with tartar sauce, shredded lettuce and sliced tomato. A piece of N'awlins just waiting to happen!*

# Tangy Lemon Broiled Fish, *submitted by Jennifer Chism*

*"Oh, be still by sole!" Jen found this recipe on the label of a designer tie. You never know where you're going to find a good recipe.*

3/4 cup salad oil

1/2 cup lemon juice

1 teaspoon dried leaf thyme

1 teaspoon dried parsley

1/2 teaspoon hot sauce

1 1/2 pounds fresh fish fillets (sole, flounder, haddock, trout, whiting)

In a shallow bowl, combine all ingredients except fish. Add fish and marinate in refrigerator 2-3 hours, turning occasionally.

Arrange fillets on broiler rack and broil about 6- 8 minutes, brushing with marinade once or twice during broiling. When fish flakes easily with a fork, it's done. Serve with lemon wedges.

Serves 6.

# Trout Amandine

*In my book, Rainbow trout is the best. It's the only trout that actually stays in fresh water all its life. It has a pink flesh similar to salmon. Leave the saltwater trout for others. When fried fish is not on your diet, this is a good alternative to battered deep fried fish. Simple yet elegant to eat.*

2 pounds freshwater trout fillets, skinned

1/2 cup butter, divided

4 Tablespoons sliced almonds

4 teaspoons lemon juice

1 teaspoon chopped parsley

In a large skillet over medium-high, melt 1/4 cup of butter. Cook trout about 3 minutes on each side until golden brown and cooked through. Remove to platter and place in warming oven. In the same skillet, melt remaining butter and sauté almonds until golden brown, stirring occasionally. Add lemon juice and stir till heated through. Pour over trout. Sprinkle with parsley.

Serves 4.

# Tuna Cakes

*As a newlywed, I prepared tuna croquettes, neatly shaped little pyramid mounds of tuna, bread crumbs, egg and seasoning. They didn't hold together very well and from what I remember they were difficult to brown on all sides and I never cooked them again. I was such an inexperienced cook back then that I never even thought about shaping them into patties!*

2 cans (6 ounces each) chunk light tuna, packed in water, drained

1 box stuffing mix for chicken

1 cup shredded mild cheddar cheese

1/2 cup shredded carrot

1/3 cup mayonnaise

2 Tablespoons sweet pickle relish

3/4 cup water

1 Tablespoon olive oil

In a mixing bowl, combine all ingredients. Mix well. Cover and chill a minimum of 30 minutes. (The chilled mixture becomes firmer and easier to handle). Divide mixture into 4 equal parts. From each quarter, form 3 thick patties. Heat 1 tablespoon of olive oil in a large skillet over medium-high heat. Pan fry the patties on both sides till golden brown (adding more oil and cooking the patties in two batches if necessary). Makes 12 patties.

Serves 6.

www.ingramcontent.com/pod-product-compliance
Lightning Source LLC
LaVergne TN
LVHW091321080426
835510LV00007B/589